About Turn

First published in 1986 by Pluto Press Limited,
The Works, 105a Torriano Avenue, London NW5 2RX
and Pluto Press Australia Limited, PO Box 199, Leichhardt,
New South Wales 2040, Australia. Also Pluto Press,
51 Washington Street, Dover, New Hampshire 03820 USA

Text © 1986 Bill Evans
Photomontages © 1986 Peter Kennard

7 6 5 4 3 2 1

90 89 88 87 86

Designed by Roger Huddle
Set by Spectrum Typesetting, London
Printed and bound in Great Britain by David Green Printers Ltd
Kettering, Northamptonshire

British Library Cataloguing in Publication Data available

ISBN: 0 7453 0203 3

The Lucas Aerospace workers' Combine Committee's plan for the manufacture of socially useful products has served as a model for arms conversion projects all over the world. Shown in a photomontage on the front cover is the prototype road-rail bus built from the workers' plan.

About Turn

The alternative use of defence workers' skills.

Text: Bill Evans
Photomontage: Peter Kennard

in association with the Greater London Conversion Council

Pluto Press

Foreword

Over one million people in Britain are dependent for their jobs on government defence spending – some 90,000 of these in London alone. How secure are their jobs? What will happen to them if the growing awareness of the threat of nuclear holocaust leads to major changes in defence policy?

This book exposes the myths that defence workers are safe under the present government. Although defence spending has been increased by almost a third (in real terms) since 1979, the number of people employed as a result of defence spending has fallen.

This year for the first time since 1979 the defence budget has decreased in real terms – and recently published government spending plans show further decreases in the future. This comes at a time when major programmes such as Trident will be absorbing an increasing part of the defence equipment budget – squeezed from these two directions many more jobs will be lost.

There *is* an alternative. We believe that diversification and planning can solve this dilemma. We are not campaigning for increased defence expenditure. In the long term, as this book shows, high defence spending damages our economy and costs us more jobs. Even this government has been forced to recognise that defence spending cannot continuously increase while schools and hospitals are being shut for lack of funds. But neither do we accept that defence workers, and their irreplaceable skills can be thrown on the scrap heap.

In the 1970s the Shop Stewards at Lucas Aerospace, a company involved in the production of components for military aerospace, decided to take positive action against the redundancies which were being forced on them. The workers drew up a detailed 'Alternative Corporate Plan' suggesting socially needed products on which they could work instead of joining the dole queue.

Their ideas were feasible, practical and profitable. Their initiative inspired trade unionists throughout the world. Any group of defence workers, in any country, can draw up similar plans.

The Greater London Conversion Council, an independent organisation set up by the GLC to look at these problems, has produced this book to show that there is an alternative to wasting skills and resources on the dole queue.

Michael Ward, Chair of the Industry and Employment Branch of the Greater London Council, and of the Greater London Conversion Council.

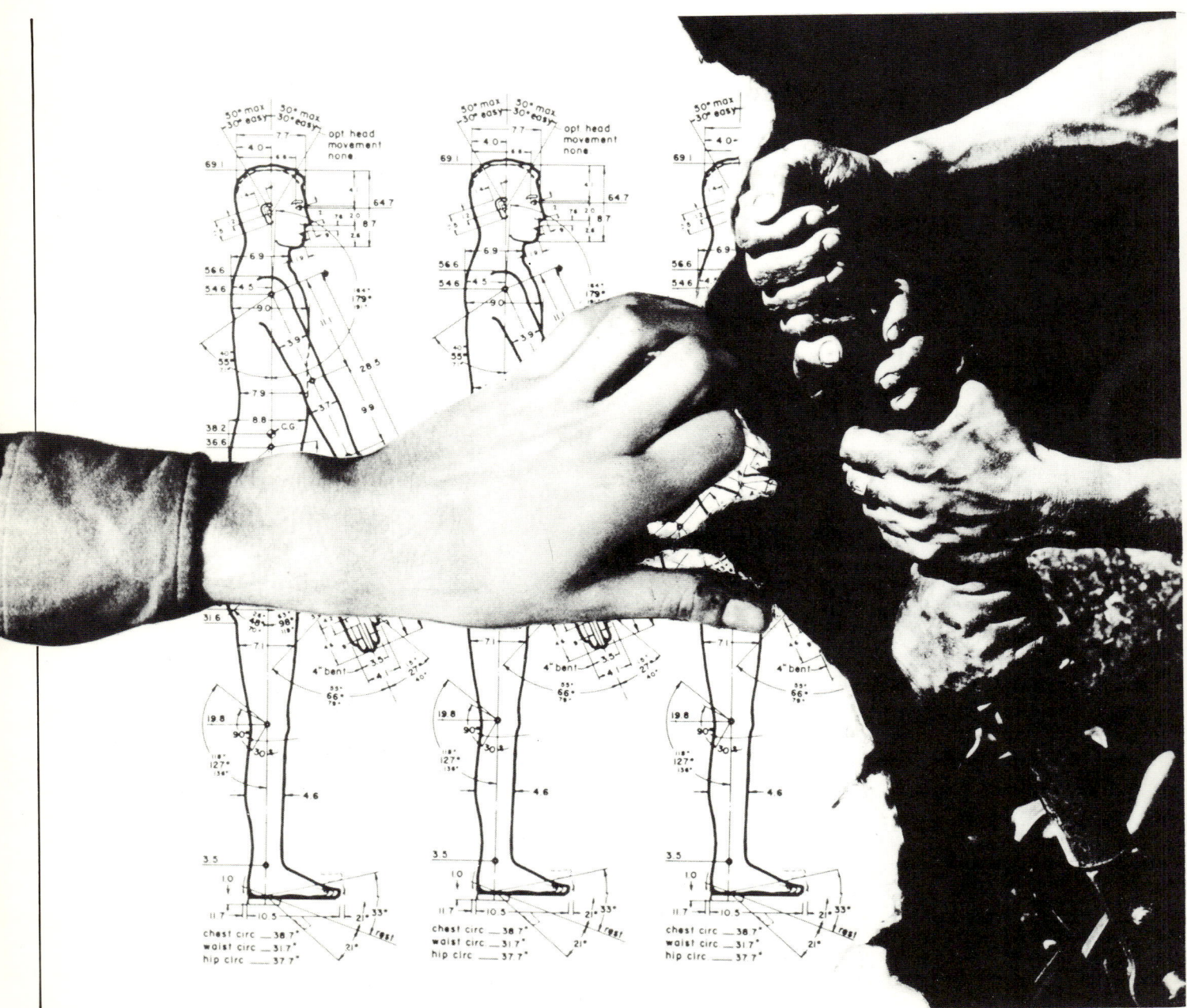

Beneath the present plans: a working future

Introduction.

Defence expenditure in Britain has risen by nearly a third in real terms since 1979, yet during this same period the number of defence related jobs has significantly declined. Defence spending now stands at £18 billion. Despite this, jobs in the defence industry remain under considerable threat.

In January 1986, the Government's Expenditure White Paper outlined its defence spending commitment for the next three years, in real terms it will mean a cut of about 5%. This is happening at the same time as the Government defence procurement policy is reducing the number of guaranteed-profit contracts for equipment and increasing competitive tendering. This encourages manufacturers to reduce their workforces. A large part of the defence equipment budget is concentrated on large complex and therefore expensive systems. These systems are vulnerable to cancellation for political and technical reasons, making jobs dependent on them especially insecure.

There is an alternative which would enable us to keep these skills and resources working for the country. It is called arms conversion. Arms conversion means diversifying military production into civilian production whilst developing and maintaining a credible defence policy — it is also referred to as product diversification. It offers an exciting opportunity which would benefit us all. The teams of workers whose skills have been practised and built up over many years could be kept together. They could turn their experience over to researching, developing and building much needed new technologies for industry, as well as new products and new services to revitalise our decaying manufacturing base. Arms conversion is the process of planning and implementing these changes.

Many trade unions have policies in favour of arms conversion. Such is the interest in the subject by trade unionists that in 1984 a National Trade Union Defence Conversion Committee was formed. The TGWU, GMBATU, AUEW-TASS, IPCS, SCPS, ASTMS and UCATT are all affiliated to it. This committee will act as a campaigning forum for better job security through conversion. As a contribution to this debate, this book will look at the effects of military spending on the economy and on jobs. It will then go on to give examples of how Britain and other countries have successfully achieved arms conversion in the past. It will show how defence workers have drawn up comprehensive plans to utilise their existing skills and resources to defend their jobs by making useful goods and meeting society's needs.

Part one.

Military spending: the threat to the economy and jobs.

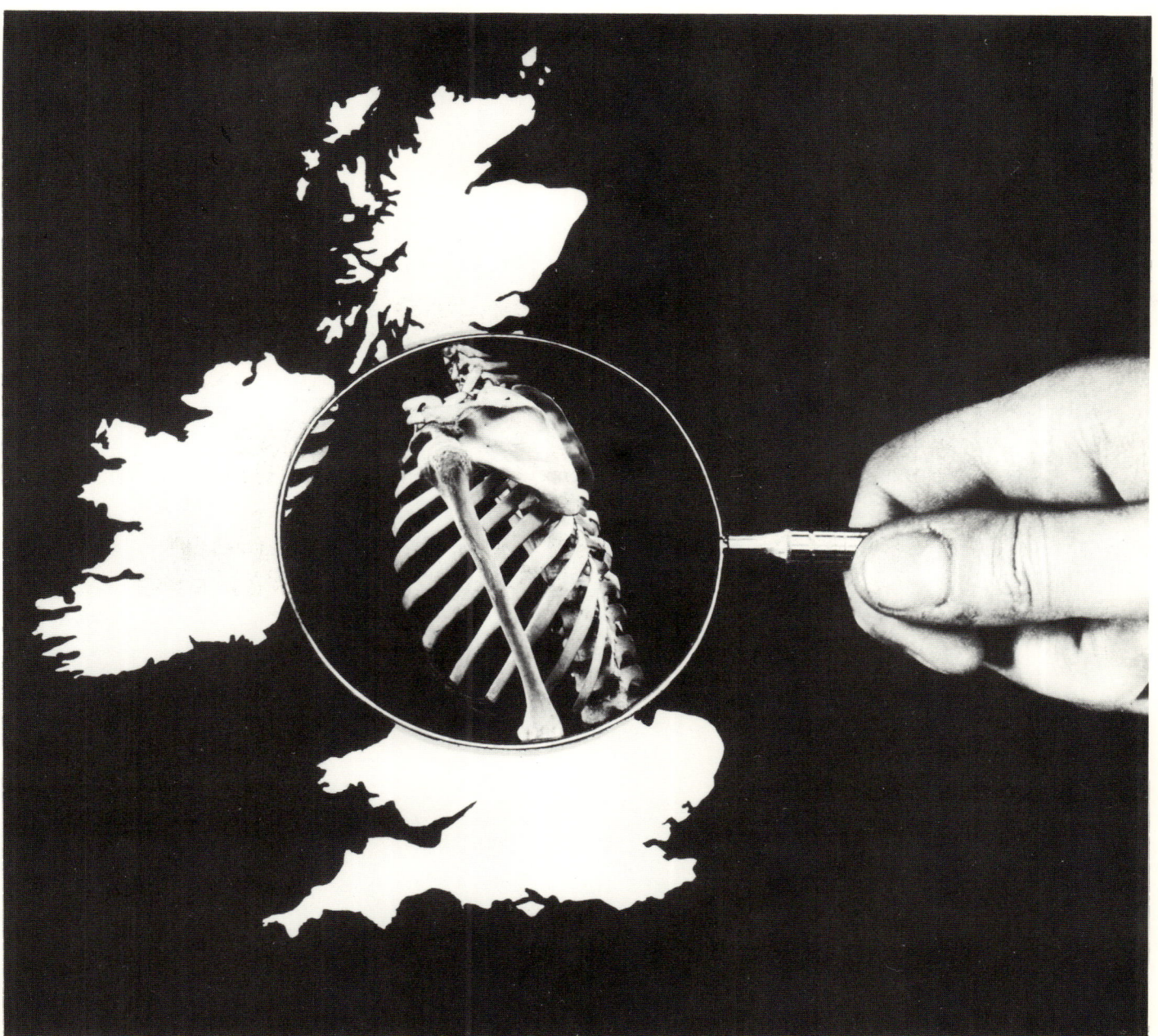

The defence budget.

The Government will spend about £18 billion on defence in 1985-6. This is:

● Over twice what it spends on trade, industry, energy and employment combined.

● About £2 billion more than its spending on health and personal social services.

● Over five times what it spends on housing.

● About £4 billion more than on education and science.

● Eight times more than it spends on overseas aid.

The £18 billion spent on defence is about 5.3% of GDP (Gross Domestic Product – a measure of total output). Of our NATO partners only the US and Greece spend a higher proportion – the European average being about 3.5%. This reflects the high priority given to defence spending by the current British Government. Military spending competes with spending on civilian plant and machinery. Without investment, plant and machinery become old and inefficient, making Britain less competitive and slowing down our economic growth.
Statistics show that countries which devote a large share of their GDP to military spending, such as Britain and the US, have a lower rate of growth than those which spend less on defence, such as West Germany and Japan.

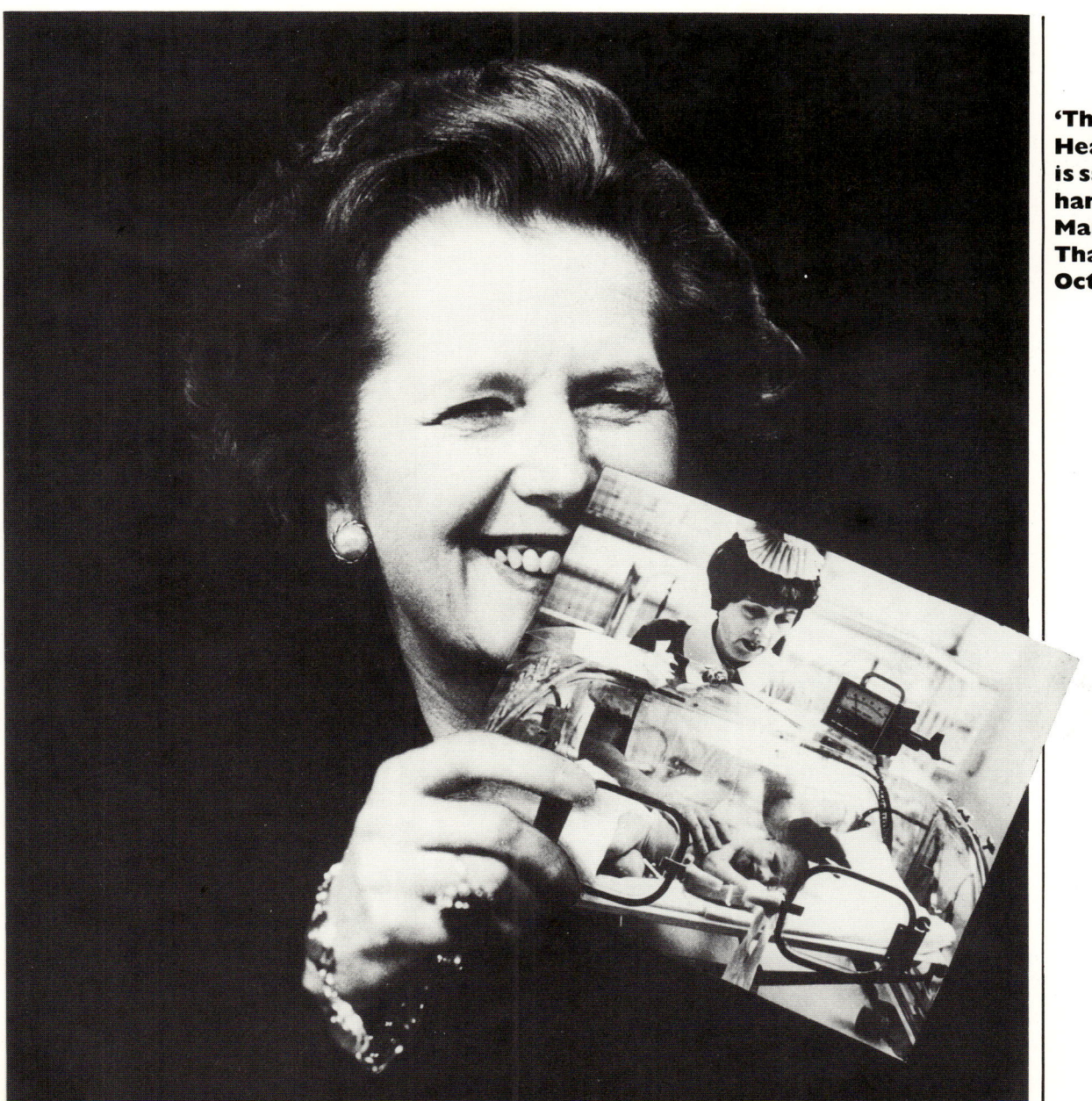

'The National Health Service is safe in our hands', Margaret Thatcher 8 October 1982

Defence spending: exploding the myths.

The government claims that this high level of defence spending enhances our security. This claim is rejected by many people who cannot accept that in times of peace so many of society's needs should go unmet. There is little point in devoting so many resources to defence if the very society we are trying to protect is seriously undermined by industrial decline.
Ample evidence also exists to show that frequently asserted claims that defence spending stimulates the economy, increases the demand for goods, helps raise living standards and accelerates technical progress are distorted and false.

The value of the pound seen through the reducing glass of military spending

A question of priorities.

"...the Government, that is me the taxpayer, buys Harrier jump jets and medical equipment like kidney machines. Lucas say it's profitable to produce Harriers but not profitable to produce kidney machines. People are dying because there aren't enough kidney machines to go round. We collected pennies on street corners and in pubs because the National Health Service couldn't provide one. The money was raised in no time. I wonder if somehow things were reversed and it became profitable to produce kidney machines and unprofitable to produce aircraft, how many people would give pennies to government ministers or civil servants on street corners when they wanted a new Harrier or Tornado?"...A Lucas Aerospace worker.

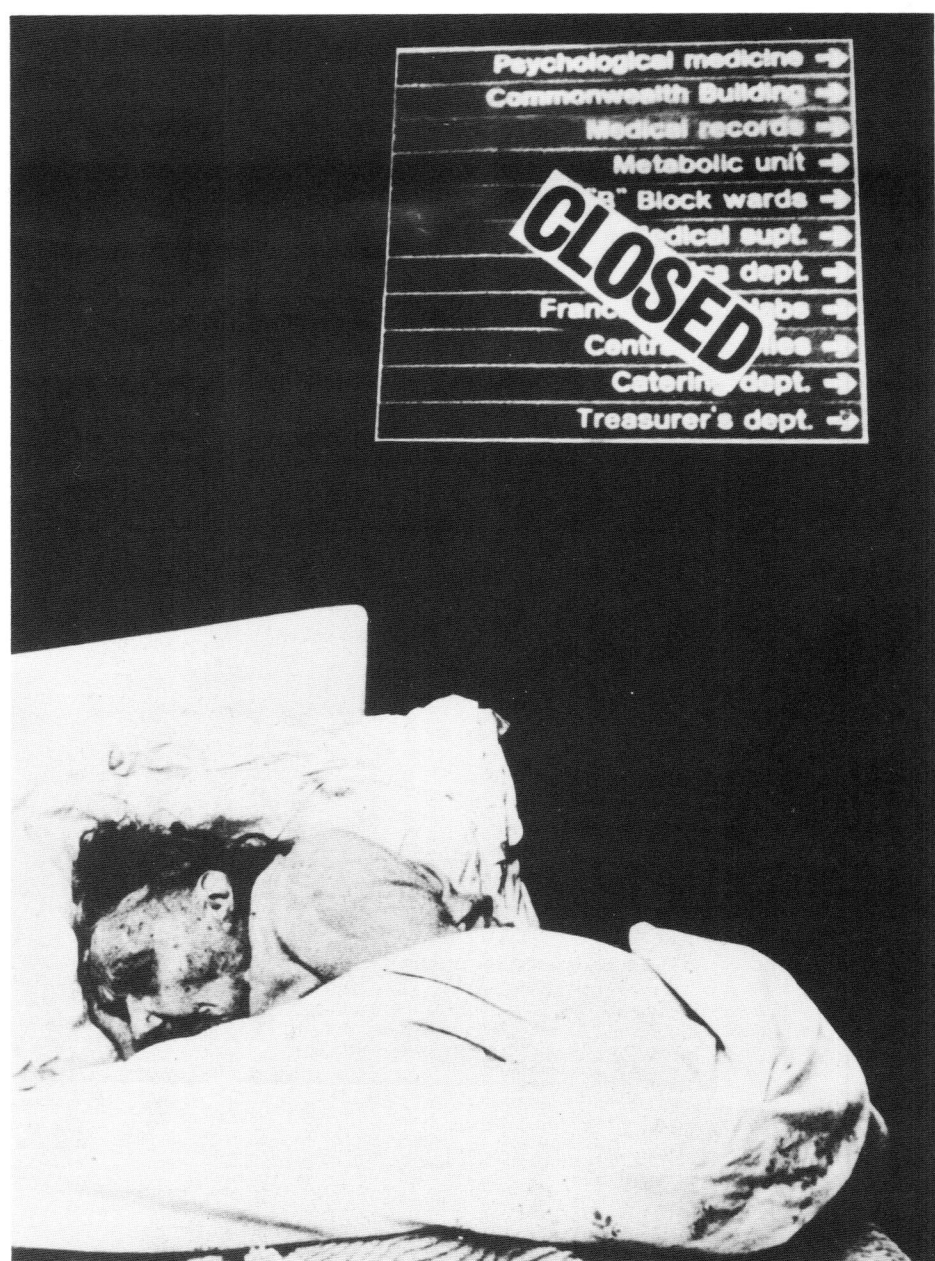

...schools...

Hospitals...

...or profits for the multi-nationals?

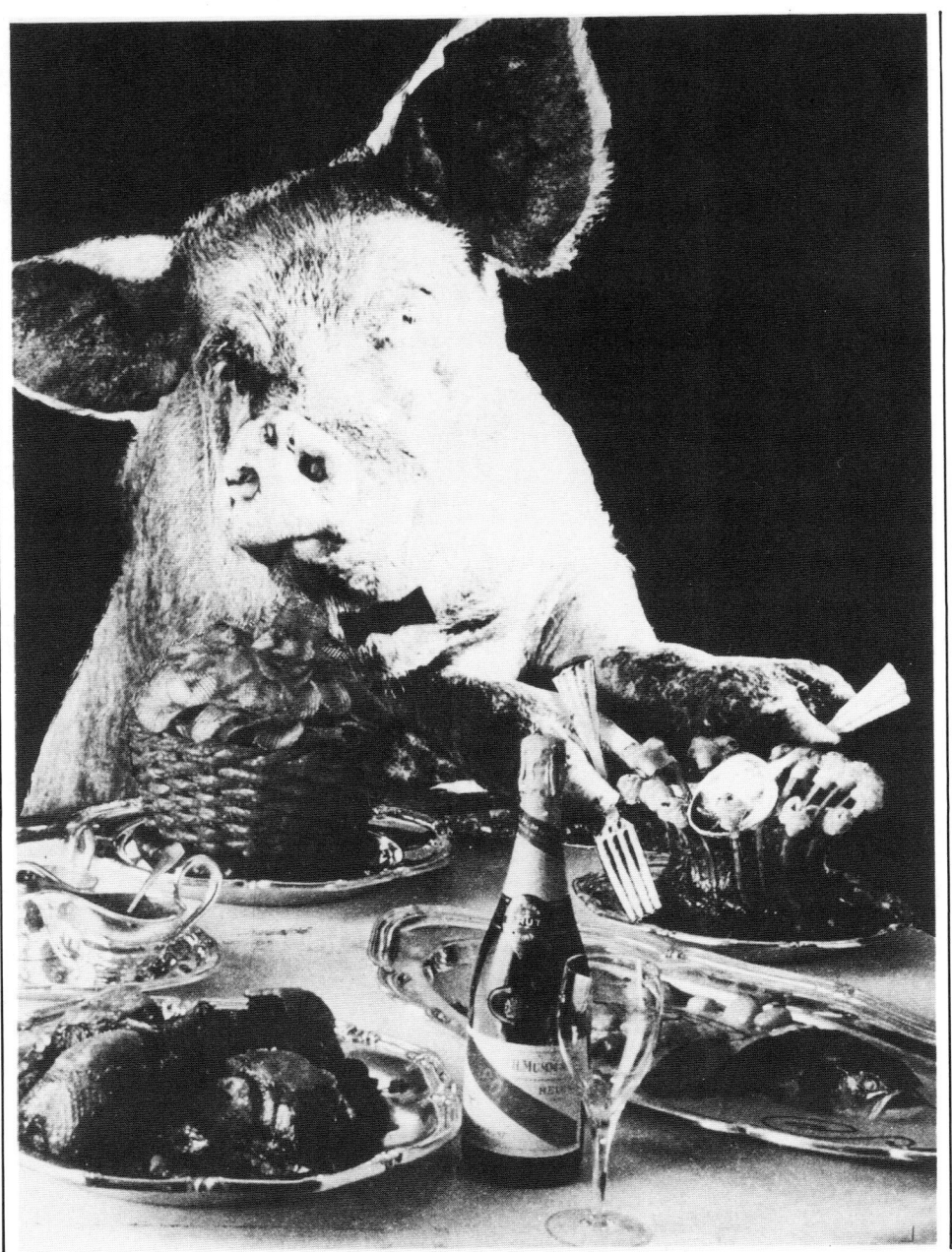

Defence spending costs jobs.

Since 1963 there have been massive increases in defence spending, and in the proportion of the defence budget being spent on equipment – in the last ten years alone this has risen from 34% to 46%. Yet since 1963 about half a million (30%) of defence dependent jobs have been lost, largely because the defence industry is a highly capital-intensive industry.
According to the government's own statistics, since 1979 over 58,000 civil service jobs have been cut (and almost 20,000 more have been transferred to the private sector in preparation for the privatisation of the Royal Ordnance Factories). The government intends to cut the civil service workforce by almost a third between 1979 and 1988.
Without planning for product diversification many more jobs are at risk in the next few years. Since 1979 this government has been committed to increasing the defence budget by 3% p.a. (in real terms). This commitment is now ended and their 'Future Spending Plans' show that the government intends to effectively cut the defence budget each year. This comes at a time when several major equipment programmes will all be reaching their peak expenditure years – Trident, for example, will be absorbing up to 20% of the defence equipment budget.
A major programme will have to be cancelled or other smaller projects will get squeezed out to accommodate them – either way without arms conversion planning, jobs and skills will be lost, damaging the training and technological base on which a strong economy is built.

Lost jobs, wasted skills

The economic drain.

Resources that could go into building up the equipment and skills Britain needs to have a strong economy are diverted by defence spending. It has been estimated that if Britain's arms expenditure since 1945 had been held at 3% of GDP national output would now be some 30% greater than it is.

Converting military to civilian production is not a simple matter of shifting some of the resources from Hi-Tech and 'expensive' military employment to 'cheaper' civilian work. It is about creating new high technologies for civilian use based on the existing skills and resources in the defence industries.

Britain must invest more in its stock of fixed capital (ie. industrial plant and machinery) to increase and update our manufacturing capacity. Without this investment even an abundant supply of materials, finance and a skilled workforce cannot meet an increase in demand for goods. Investment in defence manufacturing is made at the expense of investment in other areas of the economy. In 1983, a former chief scientist of the Department of Industry Sir Ieuan Maddock produced a report for the National Economic Development Office (NEDO) on 'Civil Exploitation of Defence Technology'. He argued that industrial policy should concentrate on reducing the difference in level between civil and defence technology. Some of the teams of people and resources currently engaged in military contracts could be transferred to support our decaying and out-dated manufacturing base, thereby keeping their skills in Britain and enhancing their value to society.

Japan, Germany and France, unlike Britain, all place great emphasis on supporting their key industries. Japan adopts a sector approach which is a little like some of the collaborative military projects we undertake in this country. The state enters joint funding agreements with leading companies in certain key industrial areas (such as electronics, telecommunications, robotics) and helps with the financing of projects too big for any one company to tackle on its own.

Burning away industrial assets

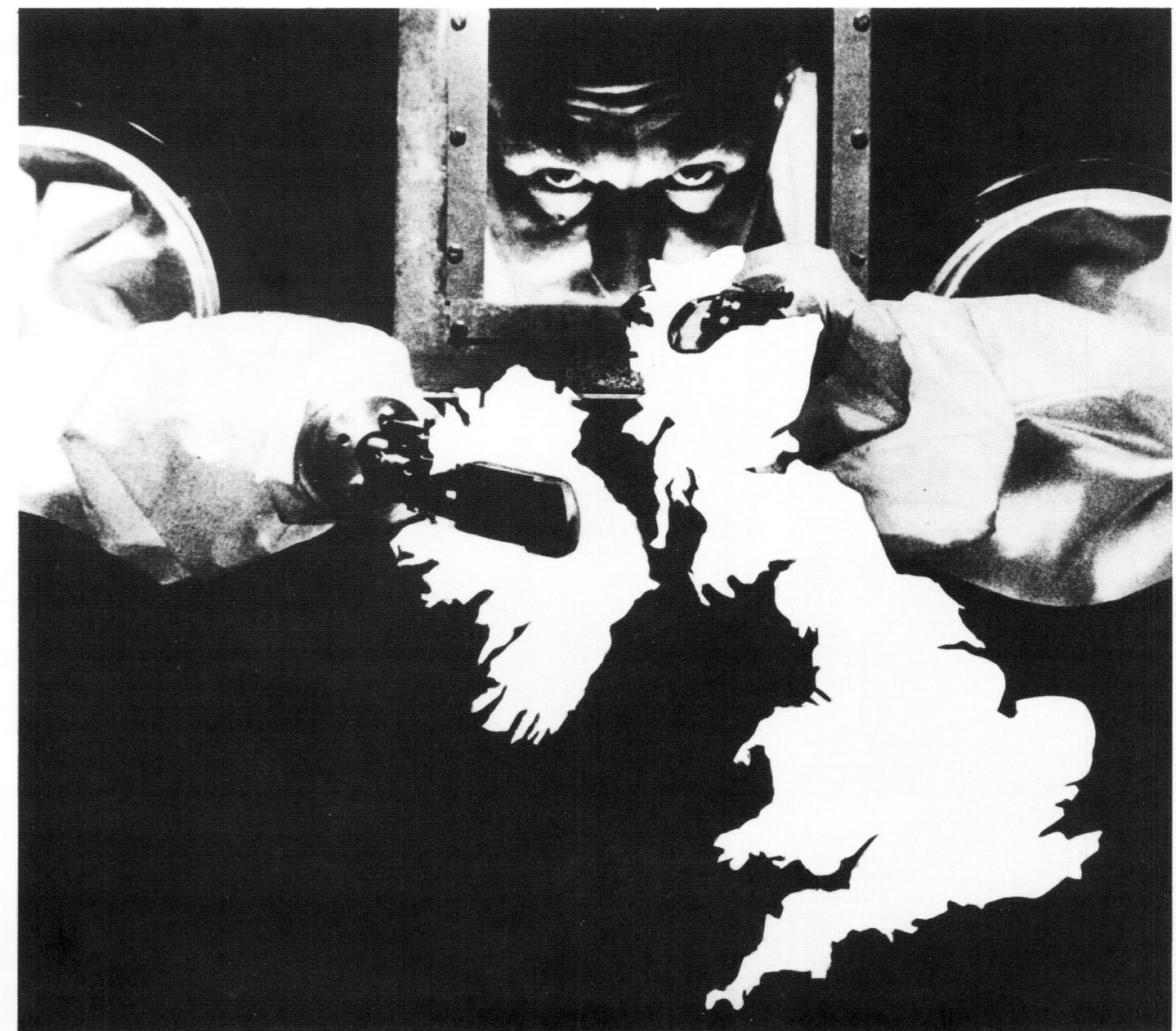

To remain economically competitive Britain must invest in long-term fundamental research and development (R&D). In 1984, the Organisation for Economic Co-operation and Development (OECD – the club of 'Western type' economy countries) drew up a report 'Science and Technology Indicators'. It looked at investment in industrial research. In terms of government funded R&D as a percentage of GDP, Britain ranked fourth in the OECD. But in fact over 50% of UK government R&D is spent on defence compared with 37% in France, 9% in Germany, and just 2% in Japan. In civilian R&D Britain drops to seventh place.

Of the OECD countries only the US spends more per capita on defence R&D than Britain. Most of our international trading partners are putting great emphasis on long-term research and development in commercial areas of fields such as robotics, bio-technology, energy, new composite materials, plastics, high-speed electronics, optical computing, and associated soft-ware development. Britain is not.

An island of military research and development

A recent TUC Report 'The Future Business' (1985), concludes that 'Britain is paying the price now for its post-war failure to match the R&D record of its competitors...unless the position is reversed, Britain will have even fewer of the new skills, the new systems, the new products with which to compete internationally in the 1990s'. Britain currently spends about £6 billion on *all* industrial research and development, almost a quarter of which is used for military purposes. This is being cut back – at a time when competitors such as Japan, West Germany and France are all increasing their expenditure – and the proportion going to defence is increasing. Already there is a shortage of skilled scientists in some of the key engineering sectors of the British economy.

The US Strategic Defence Initiative (Star Wars) programme will increase the number of high-tech corporations which are involved in military research at the expense of other developments. Although both the feasibility of Star Wars and the amount of work which will be permitted to leave the US are questionable, British companies and research establishments are queueing up to try and win contracts.

The US budget allocation is $26 billion for initial research (over a 5 year period), of which up to $1.3 billion may be available for Europe. Yet civilian spin-off from Star Wars will be very limited – space-mounted directed-energy weaponry has few obvious civilian applications.

Involvement in the Star Wars programme will hinder the long-term development of the strong economic base Britain needs by distracting even more of our limited resources from civilian fields.

The brain drain.

Reagan's brolly folly

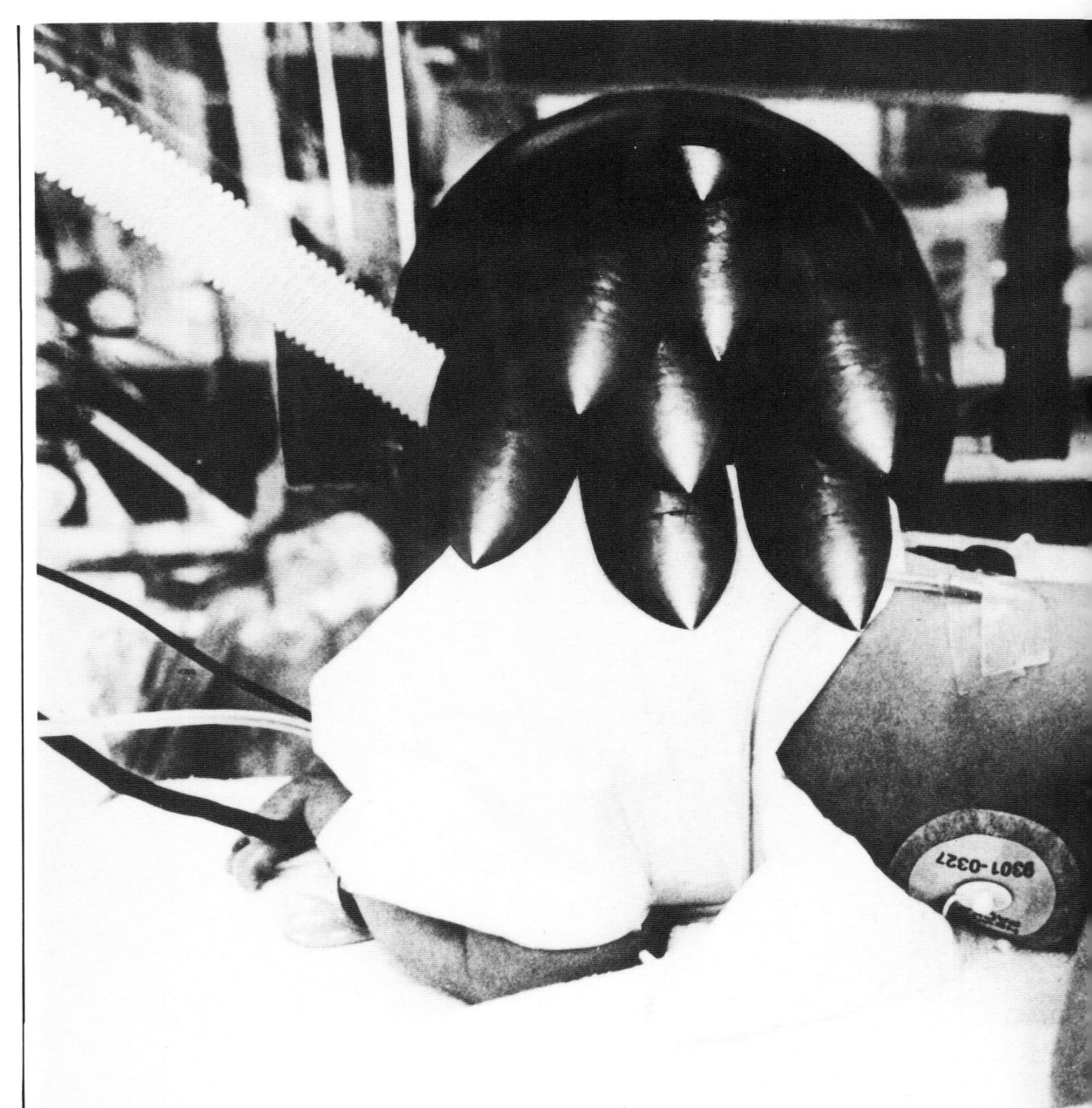

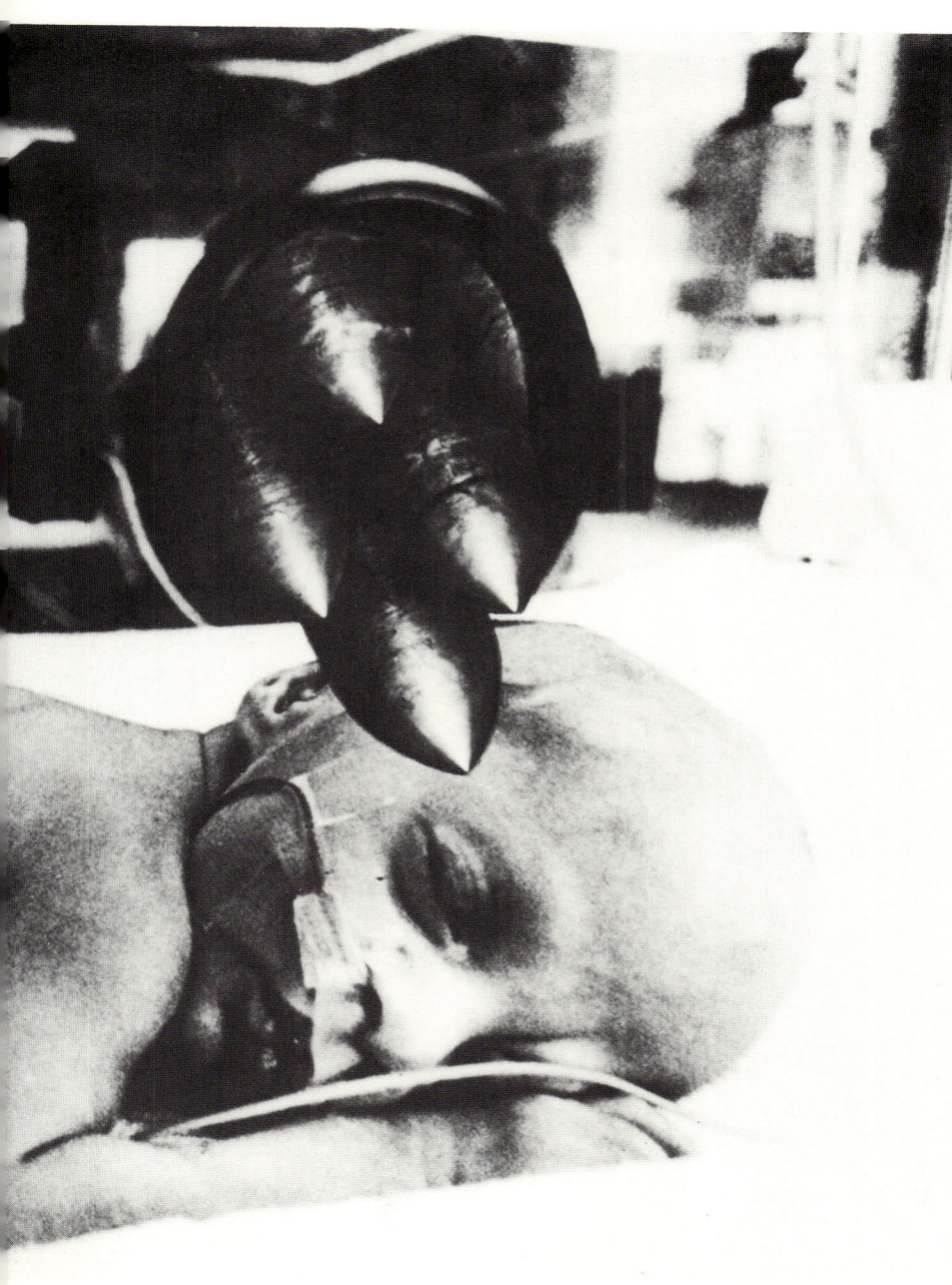

Military research and development stunts civil research and development

The international arms economy.

The scale of the global arsenal is out of all proportion to credible defence needs. Ruth Sivard has pointed out in her book, World Military and Social Expenditure (1985), that: 'the budget of the US Air Force is larger than the total educational budget for 1.2 billion children in Africa, Latin America and Asia excluding Japan. The Soviet Union in one year spends more on military defence than the governments of all the developing countries spend for education and health care for 3.6 billion people'.

Global defence spending is rising rapidly, up by a third in real terms this decade. The Stockholm International Research Institute estimated that the world would spend $800 billion on defence in 1985.

In 1981 the United Nations set up a group of experts drawn from 27 Member States to look at the relationship between disarmament and development. The Group concluded that:

● The arms race and development compete for the same resources and the world cannot do both.

● A cutback in world military expenditure of only 4-5% would enable international development assistance to be increased twofold.

● All governments should prepare assessments of the nature and magnitude of the short and long-term economic and social costs of their military preparations so that the general public in their countries can be informed of them.

So far the Swedish government is the only one to prepare such an assessment.

The fruits of our labour

The myth of spin-off.

A frequent justification for the huge sums of money spent on military research and development (R&D) is that there are substantial spin-off benefits for civilian use. This is not the case – as several reports have shown.

The 1983 Maddock-NEDO report on 'Civil Exploitation of Defence Technology' was strongly critical of the lack of commercial spin-offs, particularly from companies which have been almost wholly concerned with defence equipment for a number of years. Maddock noted that such companies possess nearly all of the technical benefits resulting from high defence R&D expenditure yet they do not transfer this technology to civilian production. He concluded that the likelihood of such firms contributing to civil areas (other than aerospace), is 'vanishingly small and even strong measures by government are unlikely to have more than a marginal effect'.

Transfer of defence technology to civilian use relies on two important interlinked factors. Firstly the technology must be appropriate to any potential application and secondly, the producers of this technology must build up a relationship with potential users of their products so as to better understand their needs. This explains the difficulty some companies find in applying military technology to civilian goods. Their technology was created as a result of the rigorous demands of the military specifiers, it was not constrained by the pricing considerations of civilian industry. For example a military company recently called in outside designers to attempt to adapt a piece of military communications equipment for the civilian market. The designers were shocked at the cost of the military equipment, until they realised that a large element of its cost was bound up in special construction for shock protection when throwing it out of the back of a low-flying aircraft.

Any chance by-products of military R&D which do occur are no substitute for advances which could be made in civil technology if some of the military resources were used for civil purposes directly.

Defence technology : useless for civil needs

Value for money?

Military products are caught up in a never-ending circle of spiralling costs. Military specifications, especially in Britain, are very demanding and rigid, leading to high cost products. Because of the high cost, fewer items of equipment can be bought. Because of this, each item of equipment has to perform more roles. Consequently, the military specifications are more demanding, the cost higher and so on. This circle is kept spinning by the very close links between the companies producing the equipment, and the MoD who are their only UK customer. Increased and enhanced features are added at high costs but to marginal advantage. This is known as 'gold plating'.

In an attempt to incorporate the latest technological advances production often begins before development is completed, this leads to design problems which require large amounts of money to solve – if they ever can be solved. For example, eleven Nimrod AEW Aircraft were ordered in 1977 in preference to the US AWACS System (which are now all in service with other NATO forces). Britain refused to participate in the AWACS on the grounds that Nimrod could be produced quicker and to a higher standard.

There have been numerous problems with the programme. The Commons Defence Committee was told by Air Chief Marshall, Sir John Rogers in 1985 that the system – already some years behind schedule, and with one-and-a-half times the original cost of £856m (1986 prices) already spent – could not be completed in less than 3 years. It will also cost between £600m and £700m more to give the RAF the capability it expected. On 22nd January 1986, George Younger, Secretary of State for Defence, announced that he was considering cancelling the project. US AWACS could be bought instead. A decision is yet to be made.

Complex technological systems tend to be less reliable than simple systems so, for instance, during the Falklands conflict the Commander of the submarine 'Conqueror' chose World War II vintage Mark 8 torpedoes to sink the Belgrano. He also had sophisticated Mark 24 Tiger Fish torpedoes at his disposal, estimated to cost about £500,000 each, but chose not to use them, probably because of their reputation for unreliability.

In contrast to all this 'gold-plated' technology which, theoretically, enables us to guide a missile from one side of the planet to another with an accuracy of a few hundred metres, blind people are still feeling their way around with a stick as they have done since the Middle Ages. There is no technical reason for this – it is simply a question of priorities.

'There is no alternative'

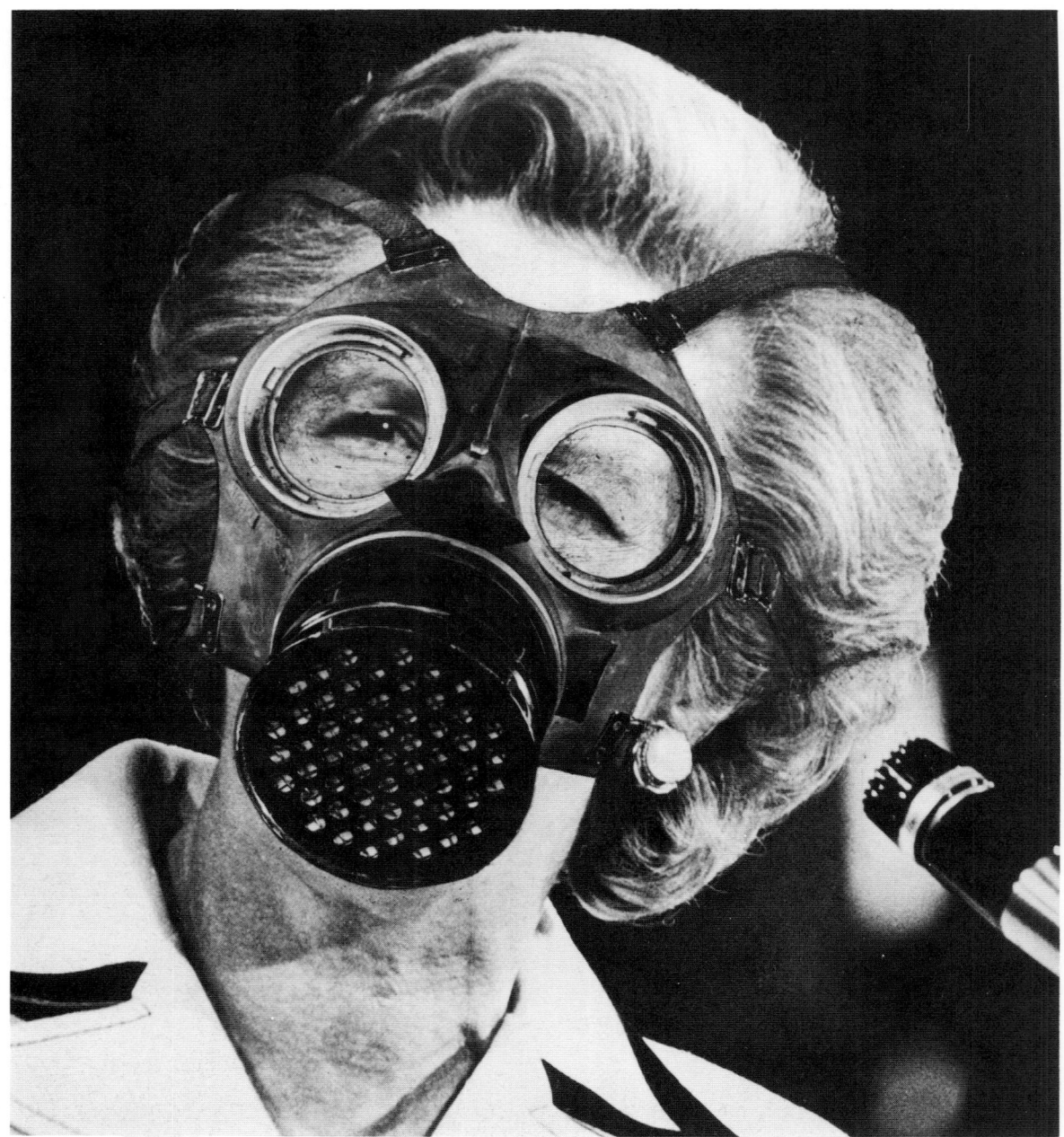

In memory of British industry

Part two.

The altern

FAC
TO
STRE

462, HOE ST.
01·539
and at 111 Lower

TORY
LET
TTONS
LEYTON, E.17.
0626
Clapton Road

Voting for a future

The opportunities of conversion and diversification.

Conversion and diversification offer an opportunity to workers in the defence industry, faced with possible redundancy, to retain their jobs and skills. It is not an attempt to stop military production, but offers a form of insurance for when contracts are lost or projects cancelled. If workers take time to plan in advance, they uncover a wealth of other opportunities. It has been achieved in the past, both here and abroad, and it must be done now to ensure the continued survival of workers jobs and to enable their much needed skills to contribute to other areas of the economy.

Conversion to a peace-time economy.

Defence budgets have been cut back much more severely in the past than any political parties are proposing today. At the end of the Second World War British defence spending was cut back from over 50% of GDP to less than 10%, although GDP as a whole increased. Millions of service personnel and munitions workers were successfully demobilised. Eight million workers were redeployed from military production in eighteen months.

Defence spending in Britain was cut-back again under a Tory government in the late 1950's. This large cut in defence spending of about 10% was again accomplished with little disturbance to the economy. Looking further afield, between 1968 and 1976, military spending in the US was cut in real terms by 35%. This caused much concern amongst the major defence unions.

They proposed a scheme that each contractor would be required to set aside a portion of their profits as a conversion reserve to be held in a government fund and released only for conversion purposes.

When proposing this plan to Congress, Walter Reuther, then president of the Auto Workers Union said "I think it is a terrible thing for a human being to feel that his security and well-being of his family hinges upon the continuation of the insanity of the arms race. We have to give these people greater economic security and greater job opportunities in terms of the rewarding purposes of peace…"

While the unions' scheme was not adopted, an Economic Adjustment Program had been initiated by the US government as early as 1961. Its main role was to supply advice and expertise to companies and communities affected by local base closure to ease them through the transition from military work to civilian work. The funds for this conversion programme are very limited and it cannot fund conversion directly, yet despite the hostile attitude in the US to planning and government intervention it is quite successful. In its first twenty years it helped to create 78,000 jobs in areas where 68,000 jobs were lost through defence cuts. For instance at Benecia, California, the closure of an arsenal and depot meant job losses for 2,318 people out of a community of only 6,450. Industrial development was initiated and 3,000 new jobs were created.

Similar examples exist at other bases around the US.

Some of these ideas have found their way into Draft legislation drawn up for Congress. A conversion Bill has never become law, but for many years there has been congressional support for conversion legislation. The draft Bills have proposed the setting up of local Alternative Use Committees consisting of representatives from the trade unions, management and the community to investigate facilities available in their defence plants. Primary responsibility for conversion planning would be vested in this committee and rely on local knowledge of skills and plant available.

A conversion fund is also envisaged by the draft Bills to provide some form of guaranteed income for people displaced, and to provide funds for conversion. Funds would be raised by a small levy on all military sales, and defence contractors would be obliged to pay into the trust as a condition of doing business.

Post war needs...

...were met by a massive shift from military to civil production

Lucas Aerospace Workers Alternative Corporate Plan.

This is undoubtedly the best known of the recent conversion initiatives in Britain. It was drawn up in the mid 1970s by the workforce of this large UK multi-site defence contractor through their Combine Shop Stewards Committee. The workforce could see redundancies and rationalisation coming and sought an alternative that would be a positive bargaining tool with which to challenge them. Its effects spread far beyond their own company, bringing the conversion debate firmly into the trade union arena. It demonstrated to other defence workers the importance of alternative plans, and questioned the nature of industrial planning nationally – showing the way for more democratic, local initiatives, and the importance of planning prior to redundancies.

The plan had many strengths. The office and shop floor assessed in detail their own skills and the resources available to them. They made 150 suggestions for alternative products which they considered to be 'socially-useful' and which used their existing skills and experience. These were channelled through the strong union organisation of their combine and used in drawing up an Alternative Corporate Plan. It was not just a shopping list of suggestions about products and markets. They were proposing conversion of existing facilities for socially useful goods. They worked on some of the products in their own time, making use of local facilities such as workshops in education establishments. Prototypes exist for the hob cart for exercising children with Spina Bifida; a road-rail vehicle and a heat pump. These all helped make the plan realistic – showing practical examples of product ideas.

The Hob Cart

The road-rail bus

Another key element of the Plan was its criticism of the market as a mechanism for allocating resources. The Lucas workers noted that arms production did not conform to 'normal market mechanisms'. They called for greater links between producers and consumers for civilian products. The plan generated much enthusiasm in the Labour movement; it created a bridge enabling workers to reconcile their campaigns against redundancy with their commitment to reductions in arms spending.
Just briefly these are some of the many product ideas from each of the five main areas suggested in the Plan – they highlight the potential of transferring the high-technology skills of the defence industry into civilian production.

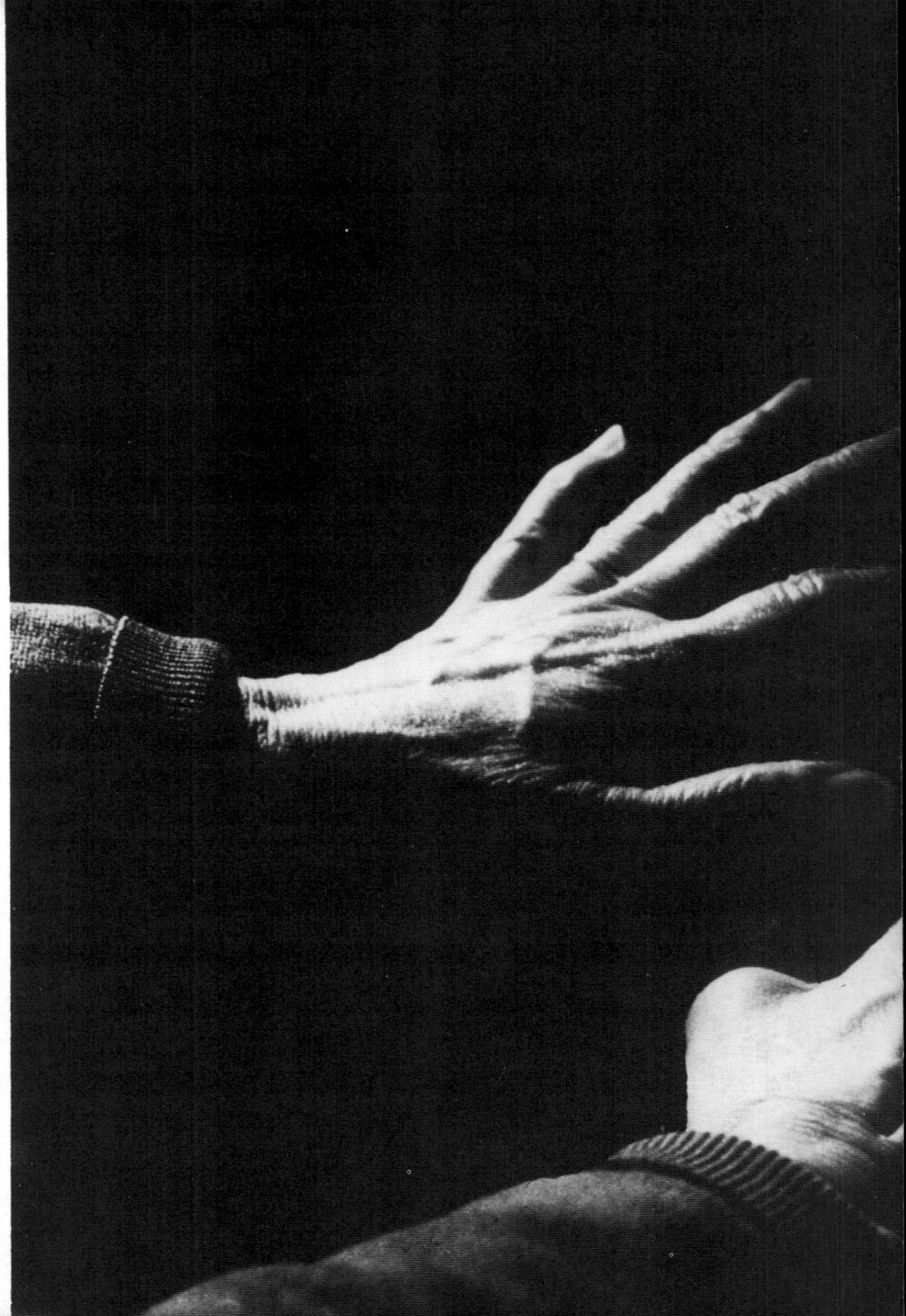

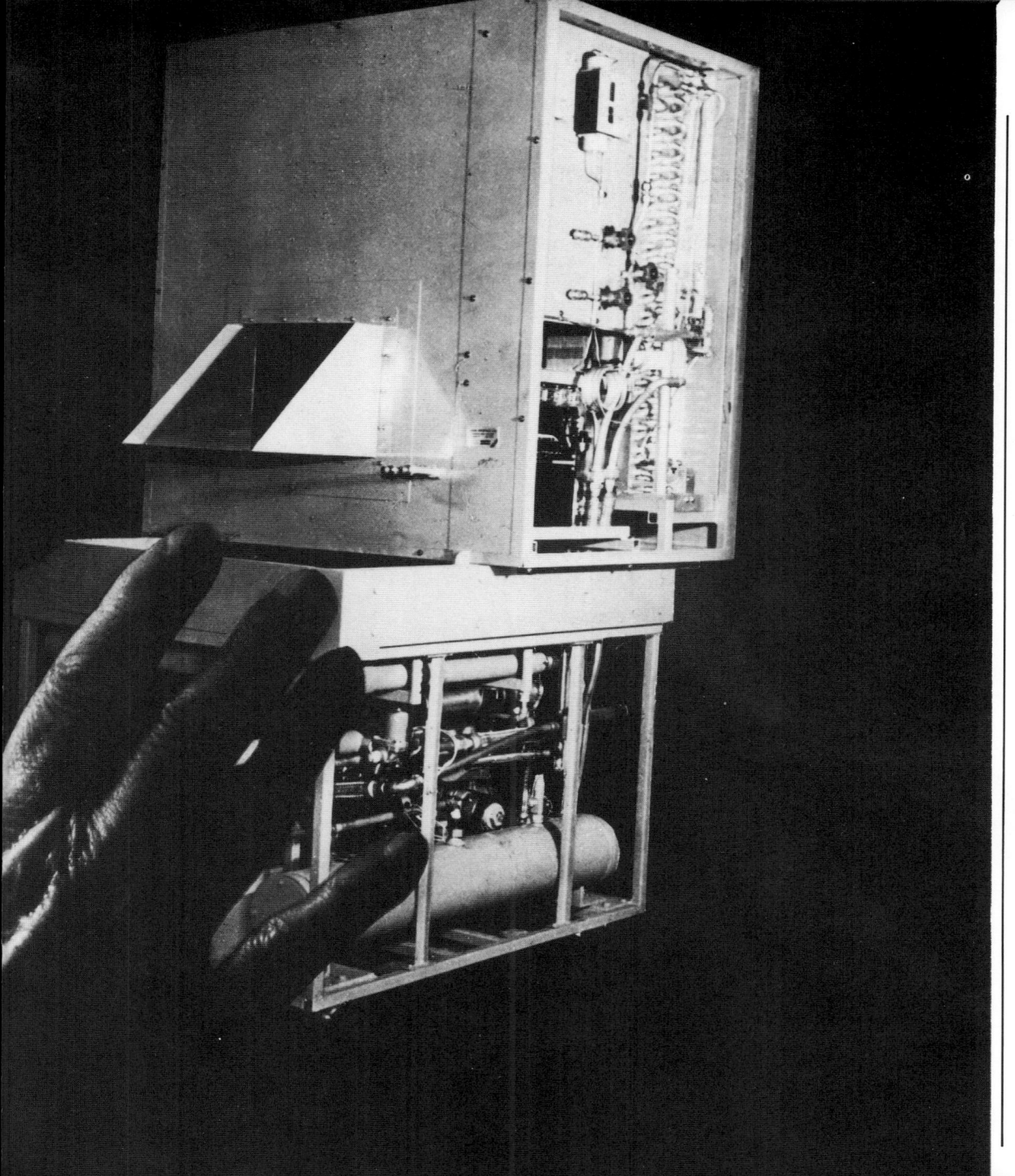

The heat pump: warming to the idea

Transport.

A hybrid power pack was suggested – combining the best use of an electric motor and an internal combustion engine – which reduced fuel consumption by about 50% and pollution by about 80%. It relied on Lucas expertise in fuel system and control. The Lucas management initially ignored this product suggestion and continued with their battery car development. But at the 1982 Motor Show a 'new' Lucas hybrid electric test car was unveiled! By this time, however, Lucas had lost the technological advance they could have had if they had taken notice of the Corporate Plan. Now most major car manufacturers in the world have developed similar vehicles.

Energy.

The efficiency of home-heating can be doubled by use of a heat pump (it acts like a refrigerator in reverse). It can be especially useful in, for example, Local Authority Heating Schemes. Lucas used to manufacture electric heat pumps but had not developed the line. The Corporate Plan took the idea of the heat pump one stage further, suggesting it be driven by gas rather than by electricity. This product had immense market potential but, as with the rest of the Plan, the Lucas management refused to consider it, in this case even going so far as to suppress one of their own company reports identifying a large potential market. Gas-fired heat pumps are now readily available 'off the shelf'.

Marine Technology.

The plan proposed that Lucas skills in mechanical and electronic controls could be used to make working in hazardous deep water environments safer. It would do this by creating Telechiric devices that enabled workers to operate sophisticated remote control extensions of their hands on the ocean floor. Thus the human operator would remain skilled but able to work in a non hazardous location.

Braking Systems.

Again, using Lucas skills in electro-mechanical engineering they suggested developments of regenerative braking systems for a wide variety of public transport vehicles which would make them not only safer but also more energy efficient.

Medical.

Lucas used to produce a limited number of bulky kidney machines. The Plan suggested expanding production of these urgently needed appliances and proposed designs for a sophisticated portable domestic version. It seemed scandalous to them that when people were literally dying of the need for such machines, Lucas workers were being made redundant.

The Plan radically extended the scope for collective bargaining. It challenged company policy by questioning what was made, what was invested, and how work was organised. It showed that there were many social needs for which they could make products. If resources were shifted from arms spending to civilian production, job security could be improved and skills could be practically transferred to design and manufacture specific products of greater social use.

The Alternative Plan showed that conversion offers an alternative to job loss. It acted as a focus for mobilising opposition to redundancies and closure. During the time the Combine Committee was strong there were no compulsory redundancies within Lucas Aerospace. Unfortunately Lucas management refused to consider adopting the Plan and were able to outmanoeuvre the Combine Committee and gradually weaken their ability to resist redundancies.

The Combine was able to get resources from educational establishments and trust funds to establish a research centre CAITS (The Centre for Alternative Industrial & Technological Systems). The Combine also established the Unit for the Development of Alternative Products (UDAP) with the involvement of Coventry Polytechnic – UDAP provides an engineering base for assessing alternative products. CAITS and UDAP have proved very useful in helping Lucas and other workforces formulate alternative plans.

Combined heat and power: plugging into wasted energy

Other workers plans.

The Lucas Plan showed that conversion offered an alternative for workers threatened with redundancy. It spawned other plans in Britain, Europe and the United States. For example Vickers' workers at both Barrow and Elswick drew up plans for their sites. At Barrow a study of the resources used to make the ASW cruiser showed that 54 alternative types of products could be made ranging from wave & tidal power generators to submersibiles for undersea exploration, and from energy and power station equipment to furniture. At Elswick the workforce looked into alternatives to building a Chieftain Tank and outlined eight areas of work where their skills could be used. They included mining machinery, fluidised bed boilers and other energy equipment, and a re-cycling plant for domestic refuse and metals. They also suggested agricultural equipment for use throughout the world.

These plans are good, practical starts to conversion. Despite lack of co-operation from government and the companies involved they act as blueprints for positive future successes in fighting defence industry redundancies.

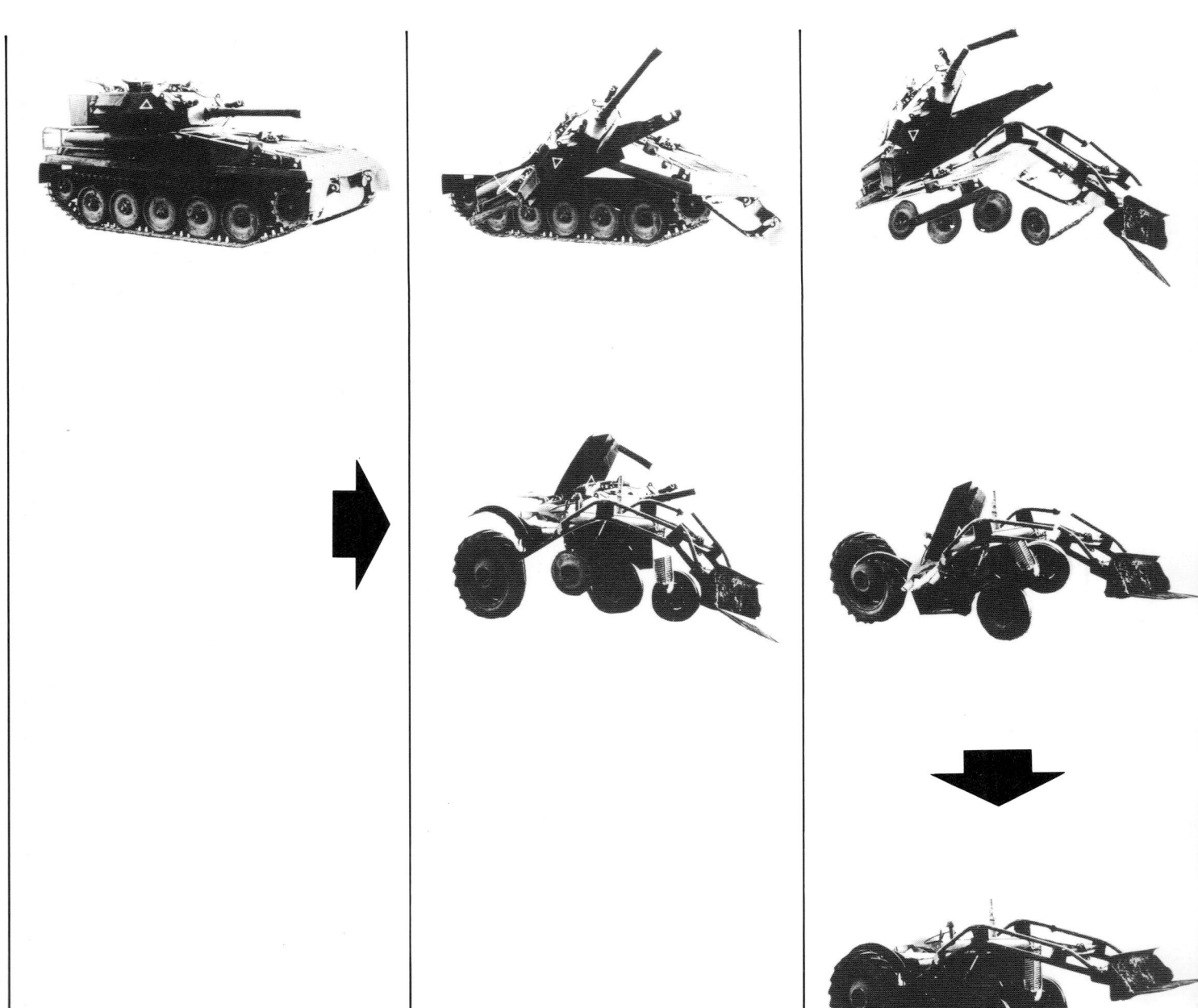

European Examples.

Waves of interest about arms conversion have spread out over Europe. In West Germany a number of Alternative Working Groups have been set up at some of the major military contractors. At Blohm and Voss workers proposed the manufacture of de-salination plants for arid areas in the Third World to replace their lost jobs in ship-building and engineering. VFW Bremen workers are examining the possibilities of making equipment for medical, energy and marine technologies. At another German firm, AEG, working groups were set up as a response to the publication of management plans for closure and mass redundancy. The groups came up with a new local transport system for Berlin based on the renovation of the S-Bahn railway and a combined heat and power plant for Berlin's district heating.

Sweden is an outstanding example of conversion initiatives in Europe. Legislation exists to prevent the defence sector dominating the economy. The Government will only award defence contracts to companies with plans for converting back to civilian production when the contracts expire. A company will normally be prevented from devoting more than 20% of its production to armaments and grants are given to encourage diversification. Saab-Scania and Volvo Flyg-Motor, who jointly will be making the new J.A.S. military plane, looked into making a new Swedish civilian aircraft to fill the gap prior to the scheduled military order. A similar exercise was undertaken at Boffors who manufacture light munitions. Again, they drew up their conversion plans on the basis of analysing the skills that went into their production.

A 1979 report from Swedish Unions and Management considered extending civilian production in defence industries. It identified important characteristics of Swedish firms that would enable them to successfully convert. They included:
- An Orientation towards high technology products.
- A close relation to civil products and technology.
- Existence of marketing organisation oriented towards the civil sector.
- Low level of dependance on military-related exports.

The report concluded with proposals for government help with conversion. They recommended establishing a method of public purchasing of new civilian products, manufactured as a result of conversion, similar to the established methods of public purchasing of military technology.
Many of these ideas and criteria from Sweden would apply to the UK defence industry.

Trade unions and conversion.

The British trade union movement has a policy in favour of conversion/product diversification. At the 1985 Trade Union Congress a comprehensive motion dealing with arms conversion was passed. It stated…'Congress reaffirms its commitment to a programme of arms conversion which will fully protect the employment of defence workers whilst permitting their labour and skills to be used for the production of socially useful goods and services.'

The prime concern of trade unions is to protect and further the interests of their membership. For defence workers this means extending the scope and influence of collective bargaining to include arms conversion/product diversification.

ASTMS 1983
Actively campaign for the removal of US military bases from British soil and the withdrawal of Britain from NATO;
Draw up a detailed and effective strategy for the transfer of resources from the production of weapons to socially useful production, with particular reference to safeguarding our members' jobs;
Forge active links with similar unions throughout the world.

AUEW 1984
This National Committee believes we must campaign for a reduction in the vast expenditure and wasteful production in the Armaments Industry, in order that resources can be directed into investment or research, development and production of more socially useful products.

GMBATU 1985
Congress notes the declining number of workers employed in the defence sector and the likelihood that fewer people will be employed as capital intensive projects such as Trident proceed, therefore this congress resolves to mount a campaign using jobs with peace as a general theme to illustrate the massive costs of Trident, contrasting the lack of funding for essential social services.

IPCS 1983
This Conference believes that the vast sums of money spent on nuclear armaments by the country could be better spent on more worthwhile and constructive projects in the public sector and that the talents and expertise of IPCS members working in the nuclear arms area could be rechannelled to the benefit of the British taxpayer and public.

SCPS 1983
We propose the following basic programme for the alternative use of resources currently devoted to Defence, which we believe to be essential steps for the long term protection of jobs for those currently employed in the Defence industry:-
That it be a condition of Defence contracts that each Defence facility has a local conversion planning committee, comprising representatives from management, unions and the local community. That there should be an examination of means of funding planning conversion.

TASS 1984
Campaign for a non-nuclear defence policy and world peace. Such a defence policy must be economically sustainable and meet the national interests of the British people. It should be based on British production with the arms industry making a contribution to the development of new technologies, some of which will be capable of civil application.

TGWU 1983
This Conference demands that the Union, when formulating policy on the alternative investment of Government defence expenditure for more socially useful purposes, must give full consideration to the employment prospects of the people currently working in the ministry of defence and related industries. Conference also declares its opposition to redundancies in the defence sector.

TUC 1983
Congress welcomes the wider involvement of trade unions in peace discussions, and believes that only through dialogue can there be understanding among people and peace between nations, and that workers must play a leading role in this process. Congress, therefore, calls on the General Council to initiate such discussions through international contacts and organisations on the common concerns of peace and security, and to examine joint efforts which can be made on the conversion of arms manufacturing to peaceful use.

Trident : a monument to waste

Conversion planning now.

Defence work is notoriously insecure. Blue Streak, TSR2, and the loss of many defence contracts when the Shah of Iran was overthrown are just some of the many well known examples of abrupt and extensive job loss. Especially insecure are those working on very large politically vulnerable weapons systems, such as Trident.
In 1982, John Nott, then Defence Secretary, informed the House of Commons that Trident would create 35,000 jobs during peak years, but he did not mention the many jobs which would be lost elsewhere to pay for Trident. The government has already revised this estimate to 32,000 and many of these jobs will only be temporary. Where the British Trident will create jobs is in the US – 45 per cent of its procurement costs will be spent there and when Trident enters service, maintenance and repair work will take place either 'on ship' or, for major work, in the US. At present Polaris (which Trident is replacing) is serviced in Britain – what will happen to all these jobs? Trident is so expensive (officially costing around £10 billion, unofficially much more than this) and is so inappropriate to British needs that all major political parties except the Conservatives are committed to its cancellation.

Concern over Trident is so great that there are two major conversion initiatives already established. One at Barrow, where the submarines are to be built and one on the Firth of Clyde, near Glasgow where Trident is to be based when it is operational.

Barrow Alternative Employment Committee.

A conversion initiative is currently underway at Vickers Shipbuilding and Engineering Ltd (Barrow in Furness). The yard has recently had substantial new investment, at a cost of approximately £240 million, making it one of the most modern shipyards in the world. This is to equip the yard for its monopoly production of Trident submarines and also to make the yard more attractive to potential buyers when the yard is privatised. The new owner of the yard will automatically acquire the contract for four Trident submarines. Vickers is the major employer in Barrow, with 12,000 workers out of a working population of 38,000. The Vickers works is divided into two parts, the shipyard with 8000 workers and the engineering works with 4000 workers. There is wide concern at such a heavy dependence on one military project. Terry McSorley, chair of the local Trades Council, explains 'the fear is that because Trident is politically sensitive it could be cancelled.' Because of this feeling of insecurity, shop stewards from Vickers and the local Trades Council are looking into alternatives.
They have formed the Barrow Alternative Employment Committee to look at the impact of Trident on jobs in Barrow and the possibilities of arms conversion for the yard. With a grant of £12,000 from Trade Union CND they have employed a research worker to help assess the yard's capabilities. A social and economic assessment of the shipyard and the local economy is being carried out.

A programme of research into alternative products is planned. Ideas are concentrated on marine-based technologies and heavy engineering products such as de-salination plants, and constant speed generators to improve fuel efficiency of ships. In the long-term the Alternative Employment Committee would like to see the development of Vickers as a maritime research and development centre to anticipate the commercial exploration of the world's oceans and produce tools and equipment for such activities.
Workers are also worried because the programme of Hunter-Killer submarines they were involved in has been interrupted to accommodate Trident – which is far more vulnerable to cancellation.
The Alternative Employment Committee has the support of all the trade unions organised in the Barrow yards as well as local, regional and national backing.

The Alternative Economic Study Group (AESG)

The AESG was set up in 1984 as a result of local concern about unemployment and dependence on the Ministry of Defence as a major employer in the Dumbarton and Rosneath peninsula on the Firth of Clyde near Glasgow. The Royal Navy maintain two bases in the area: the Royal Naval Armaments Depot at Coulport, where Polaris nuclear weapons are stored and the proposed site for storage of Trident missiles; and the Clyde Submarine Base at Faslane, the operational submarine base for Polaris and proposed base for Trident.

The Group, based in premises provided by Dumbarton District Council has the broad support of the local community, including the District and Regional Councils, and employs a full-time worker. Trade unions involved include the local Trades Council and the TGWU (which has the majority membership at the establishments involved). The group is also supported by local peace groups, political parties, church groups and MPs.

In April 1985 the group published a major survey, 'Polaris and Trident – the Myths and Realities of Employment'. The report details the dependence of the area on defence spending and in particular on Britain's 'independent' nuclear deterrent.

The report analyses the growth of the Clyde Submarine Bases and their effects on the local economy. It details the local skills available and looks at the future of employment in the area with different spending options, for example, continuing with Polaris; replacing with Trident; decommissioning Polaris and cancelling Trident; or total base closure. It concludes that Trident will not create any new long term jobs in the area.

This detailed information makes the report an ideal foundation from which to build conversion plans.

The AESG is important because it examines the links between defence expenditure and the local economy, and acts as a forum for local initiatives. The broad base of community interests involved can offer practical assistance to conversion projects within the base and local area. In the words of Iain Macdonald, Chair of the AESG, "Civilian employment within the defence sector and military bases is likely to decrease whatever government is in power and therefore a major effort must be made to establish viable alternative sources of employment". The work of the AESG is one step towards this.

Llangennech

This Welsh Naval Stores Depot is under threat of closure, the Ministry of Defence claiming that this could save on average £3 million per year over eight years. This figure is widely disputed and as a result of pressure from a Joint Action Committee, consisting of eight trade unions on the site, they have succeeded in postponing the MoD's plans. The Joint Action Committee is still successfully fighting the closure but as an extra precaution they are also looking at other alternative uses for the site.

The workforce of 400 is approximately 60 per cent industrial and 40 per cent non-industrial. Although the site is mainly a service depot, it also has special facilities including heavy lifting gear, and various different test areas employing highly skilled technicians who make up about 10 per cent of the workforce.

The Action Committee are undertaking a skills audit, and looking at external factors, for example, Llangennech has good road communications being located on the M4 motorway. Working with support from the local community and authority they are looking at how the depot could fit into the local economic development plans, as well as its possible use by other government departments.

The GLCC explores the needs of London's defence workers

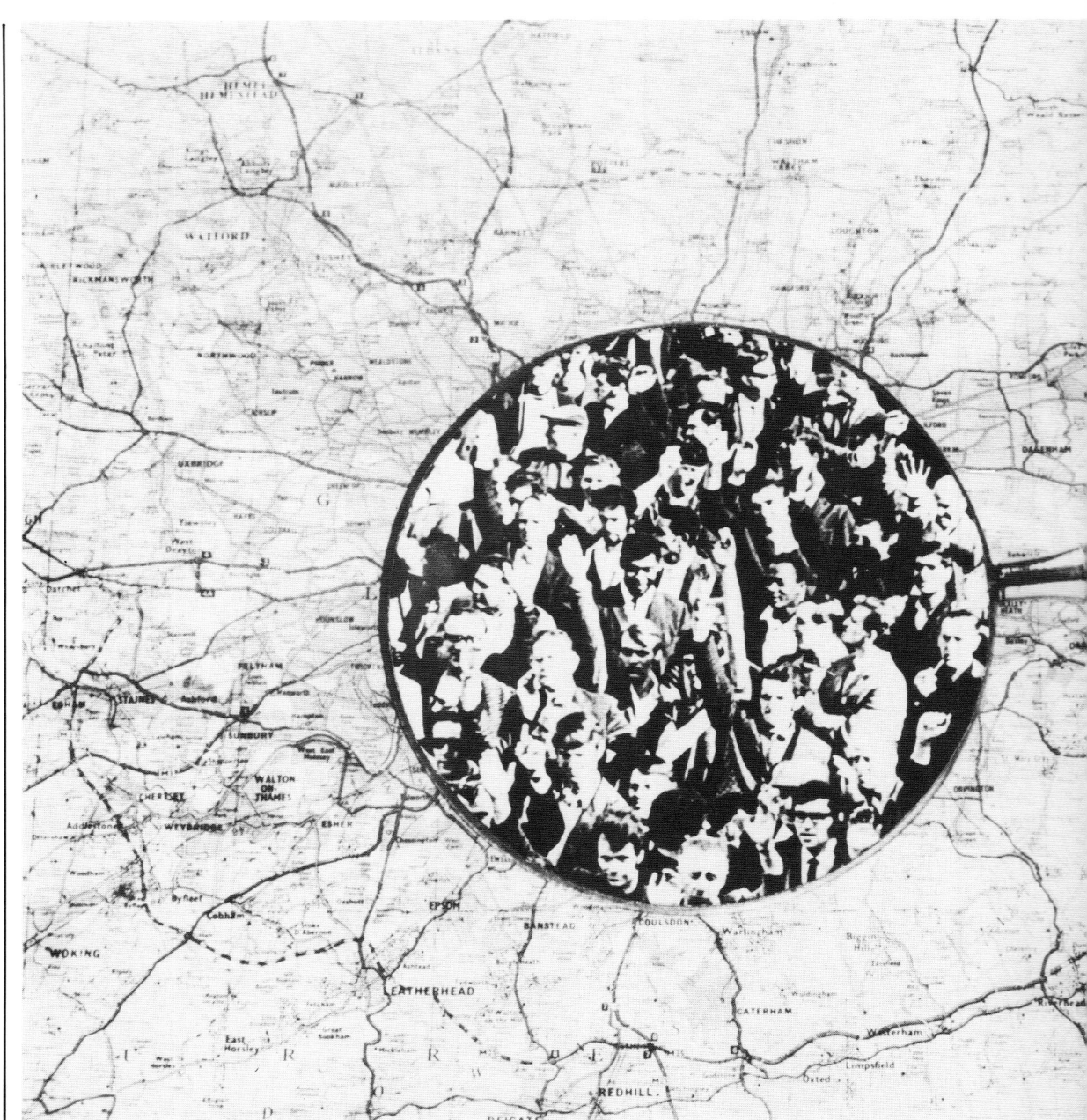

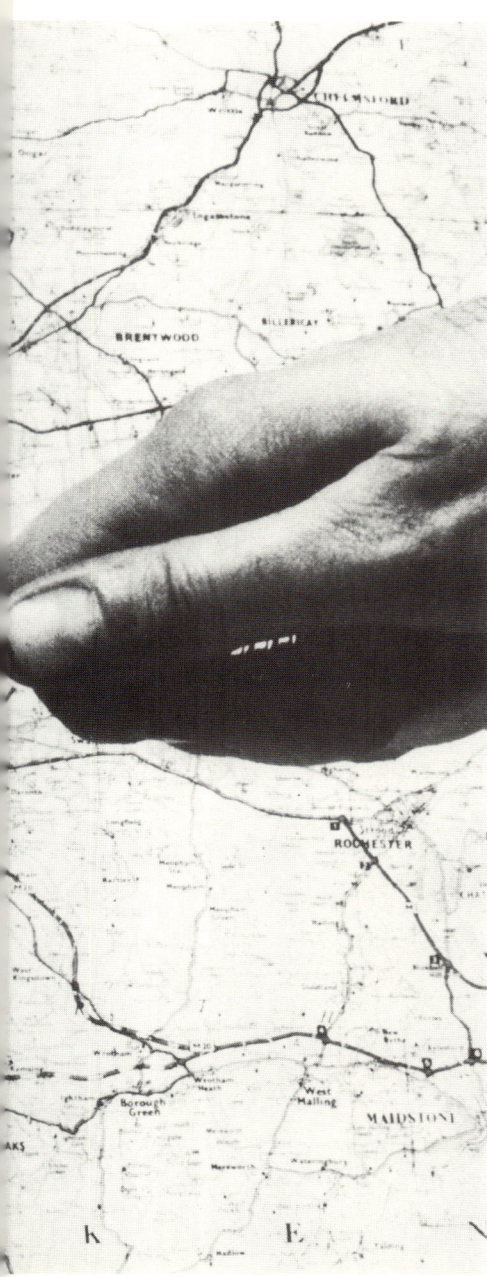

Supporting conversion initiatives.

In London the GLC recognised that planning and industrial strategy were an essential link between its policies on reducing defence budgets and protecting people's jobs. As a practical step towards this, it established an independent Greater London Conversion Council (the GLCC). Members of the GLCC include the South East Region TUC and individual trade unions, the Greater London Enterprise Board, engineers, economists and other interested organisations.

A full-time worker co-ordinates their work, which as well as publicising the need for arms conversion, includes researching London's defence sector; helping to provide advance warning of adverse trends in London's companies for defence workers; and approaching defence workers through their trade unions. The GLCC encourages workers to look at possibilities for improving job security by considering ways to reduce their company's dependence on defence contracts.

The Conversion Council acts as a forum for discussion and exchange of information and has organised conferences for trade unionists and for defence employers. It has produced reports on some of the major defence companies in London and an exhibition describing arms conversion and how it relates to London. One of the chapters in the London Industrial Strategy, the GLC's economic strategy for putting London back to work, is devoted to arms conversion.

The Greater London Enterprise Board (GLEB), an independent organisation set up by the GLC to assist London's economy, has established five 'Technology Networks' which are equipped with all the necessary staff and facilities to produce a wide range of prototypes. These Networks are not established as aloof research centres, but as practical places which work with local people developing their products.

Similar efforts are being made in Sheffield by the City Council's Department of Employment and Economic Development. For example, jointly with the Sheffield City Polytechnic they have set up an organisation called SCEPTRE to create and retain employment in Sheffield. The centre develops new products and processes, concentrating on socially useful products and techniques which preserve skills. Product diversification and planning by workers is a way of preventing redundancies in all sectors of the economy – not just in the defence industry.

These supporting initiatives coupled with research centres like CAITS and UDAP can complement the skills of the workforce when helping draw up diversification plans. They are an essential part of implementing arms conversion.

As the Lucas Plan showed all too clearly, while the best source of ideas and plans is from the workers themselves, without external help from sympathetic local authorities and preferably national government, conversion is very difficult to achieve. On the other hand the defence industry is such a large part of our key industrial sectors that it must be taken into account when drawing up local and national economic strategies.

Developing a technological network for the community...

...and not for soaring profits

Taking control of our skills to build a better future

Conclusion.

Defence workers' jobs are increasingly insecure. In the next few years the defence budget will be effectively cut back each year, and without advance planning many jobs will be lost. The political vulnerability of large weapons programmes is also threatening whole communities as local employment can become dependent on a single weapons system.

Current levels of defence spending are damaging our economy and causing under-investment, stunting economic growth, and increasing unemployment.

There is an alternative. Conversion offers real opportunities for maintaining the skills and experience of defence workers, at the same time supplying people's unmet needs. Is Britain really so well-housed and cared for that it can afford to throw people away on the dole queue? Product diversification will enable our high technology skills to be used more effectively in our civilian economy, building a stronger industrial base from which to launch greater national prosperity.

It will not be easy. Conversion will not happen overnight. Previous initiatives have shown the strength of forward planning but also the importance of policy changes by both companies and government. Workers must work together, through their trade unions, examining their skills and resources. By so doing they can open up a whole wealth of practical ideas for converting their craft through technology to alternative products.

Conversion is not an attempt to stop military production but offers a form of insurance for when contracts are lost or projects cancelled. Planning for conversion today can end the threat of redundancy tomorrow.

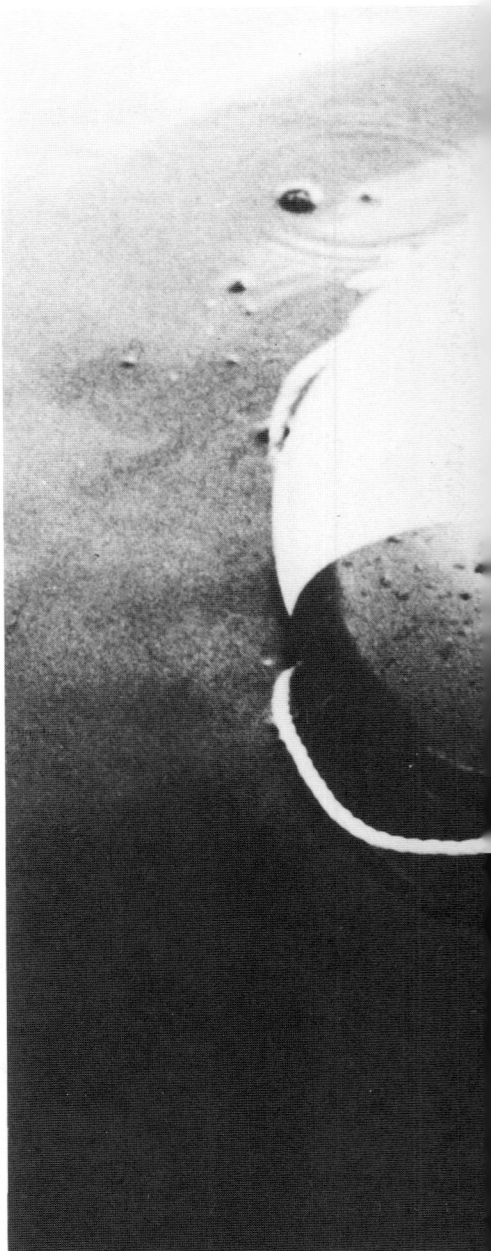

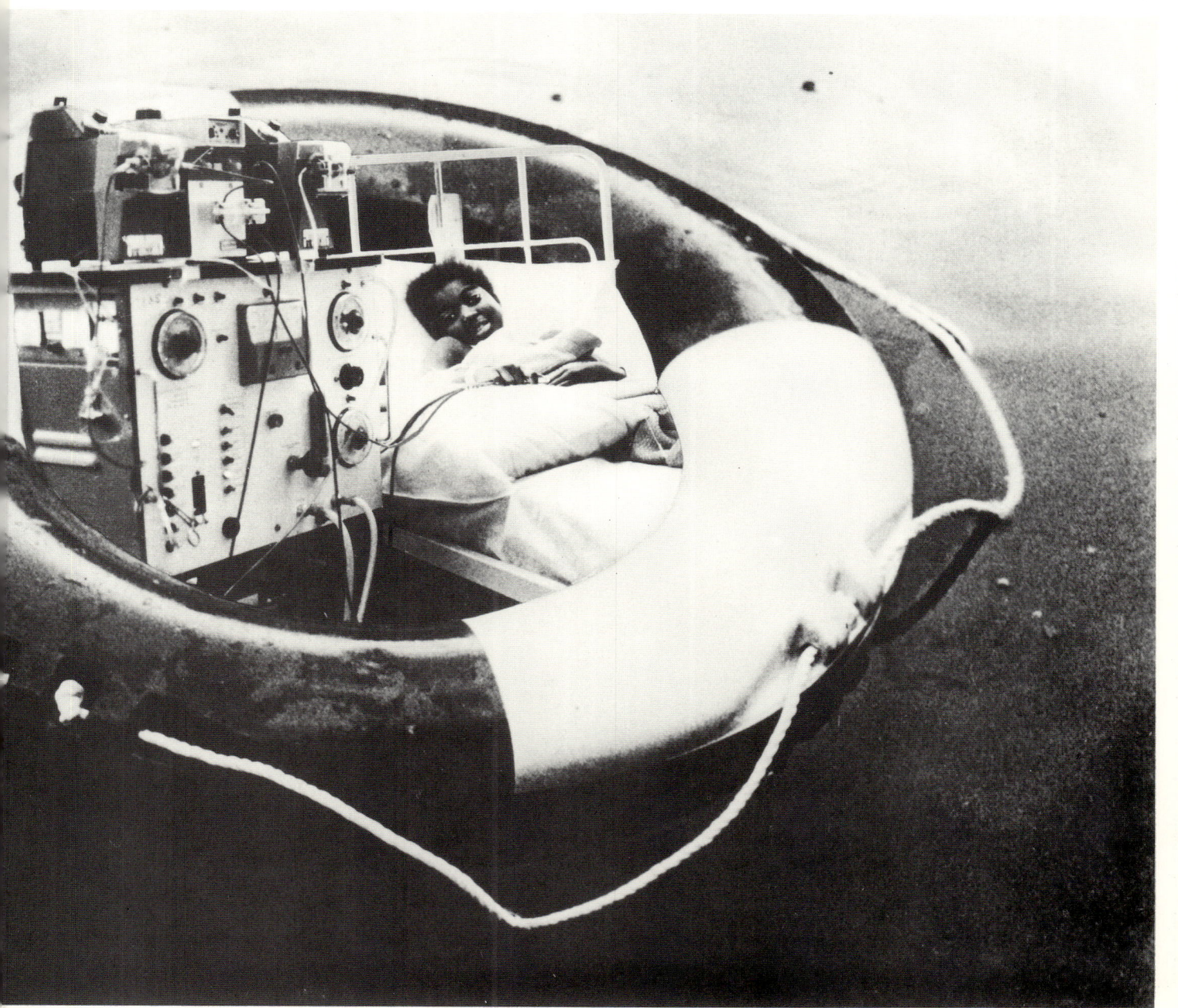

Sources and further reading

Trade Union Publications
- SCPS: *Defence Expenditure and Employment: The case for a Planned Programme for the Alternative Use of Resources.* 1983
- AUEW/TASS: *Defence and Jobs.* 1984
- IPCS: *Switching Over – Nuclear Arms, Defence Spending and Jobs.* 1985
- TGWU: *A Better Future for Defence Jobs.* 1983

Other Publications
- Alternative Employment Study Group *Polaris and Trident: the Myths and Realities of Employment* Scotland: Lomondprint 1985
- D Elliot *Defence Industry Conversion: A Review of the Options.* Open University, 1985
- M Chalmers *Paying for Defence: Military Spending and British Decline.* London Pluto Press, 1985
- M Kaldor *The Baroque Arsenal* London Abacus 1983
- Greater London Council, Arms Conversion Chapter in *London Industrial Strategy* 1985
- D Smith & R Smith *The Economics of Militarism* London Pluto Press 1983
- H Wainwright & D Elliot *The Lucas Plan: A New Trade Unionism in the Making?* London Allison & Busby 1982

Organisations

- Greater London Conversion Council, c/o GLTURU, 13-16 Borough Road, London SE1 0AL
- Greater London Enterprise Board, 63/67 Newington Causeway, London SE1 6BD
- Alternative Employment Study Group, Old Academy Buildings, Church Street, Dumbarton, G82 1QL
- Barrow Alternative Employment Group, 22 Hartington Street, Barrow in Furness, Cumbria LA14 5SL
- Llangennech Joint Action Committee, c/o Keith Edwards, 50 Nevill Street, Llangennech, Dyfed, Wales
- Centre for Alternative Industrial and Technological Systems (CAITS), Polytechnic of North London, Holloway Road, London N7 8DB
- Unit for the Development of Alternative Products, Coventry (Lanchester) Polytechnic, Priory Street, Coventry CV1 5FB
- Trade Union CND, 22/24 Underwood Street, London N1 7JQ
- Armament and Disarmament Information Unit, Science Policy Research Unit, Mantell Building, University of Sussex, Falmer, Brighton BN1 9RF
- School of Peace Studies, University of Bradford, Bradford BD7 1DP

Trade Unions initials used in the text...

SCPS: Society of Civil and Public Servants
UCATT: Union of Construction, Allied Trades & Technicians
AUEW/TASS: Amalgamated Union of Engineering Workers/Technical, Administrative and Supervisory Section
GMBATU: General Municipal, Boilermakers' and Allied Trades' Union
IPCS: Institute of Professional Civil Servants
ASTMS: Association of Scientific, Technical & Managerial Staffs
TGWU: Transport and General Workers' Union

The **Greater London Conversion Council** aims to raise awareness of arms conversion and product diversification in London. It gathers information on London's Defence sector and helps provide an 'early warning service' for defence workers.

Through their trade unions, workers are approached and encouraged to look at possibilities for improving their job security by reducing their dependence on defence contracts.

The GLCC combines a broad cross-section of interests both from individuals and organisations – the South East Region TUC and individual trade unions, Greater London Enterprise Board, London Boroughs, universities and polytechnics, defence economists and other interested organisations.

If you would like further information about anything in this book, please contact:
Greater London Conversion Council
c/o Greater London Trade Union Resource Unit 13/16 Borough Road
London SE1 0AL
Telephone Number: 01-928 2002